# Shattered Yet Whole

## Poems from the heart.

Lisa Meyers

BookLeaf Publishing

India | USA | UK

Made with ❤ on the BookLeaf Publishing Platform

www.bookleafpub.in

www.bookleafpub.com

# Dedication

This book is dedicated to those who fight through the struggles of life. To the warriors who face each day with courage despite the challenges that stand in their way. It is for the individuals who, even in their darkest moments, find a glimmer of hope and press forward with resilience and determination.

# Preface

This collection is not just a compilation of poems but a journey of discovery. It is an exploration of language and emotion, a voyage into the heart of what it means to be human. Let the words resonate, stir your thoughts, and awaken your senses.

# Acknowledgements

To the reader: Thank you for opening these pages and allowing me to share my world with you. Your engagement breathe life into this collection, and for that, I am profoundly thankful.

In gratitude,
**Lisa Meyers**

# 1. Gone

Gone
Empty
Deep
Loss

Numb
Still
Confused
Shock

Silence
Busy
Reflect
Pain

Trickle
Pause
Feel
Ache

Remember
Smile
Breath
Sting

# 2. Free

Your laugh is deeply pure and free
You protect your peace openly

You are never afraid to fail
Your love is unconditional

You do exactly you want
Your skills you never overflaunt

You embrace the fun every day
You listen to all that I say

Your touch is a calming relief
Your humor is beyond belief

Your heart is deeply innocent
Your love is truly infinite

# 3. Breathe

stay present, inhale
at this moment, only breathe
ride the wave, exhale

# 4. Discomfort

No
Back
Resist
Discomfort
Hurdle
Push
Go

# 5. Blanket

5

Let the night begin
Softness on my skin
Resting on my mind
Now I can unwind
Blanket for the win

# 6. Panic

All alone in my head
Desperate in Isolation
Mental walls closing in
Yearning for a breakthrough

# 7. Heartache

Heartache deepens over the years
First time a friend will hurt you most
Pain grows, then breaks you into tears
Second time a crush will be the host
The emotional ride you must coast
Third time your love made other plans
This low you feel you can't disclose
Fourth time your last hold on their hands
Heartache deepens over the years

# 8. Family

Family
Dedication
Loving, Giving, Caring
A heart of precious memories
Connect

# 9. Fine

9

I am doing great thanks for asking
No really I am doing good
Okay I have been better
Not the worst day ever
It's just how life goes
I keep pushing
I'll be fine
Need sleep
Cry

# 10. Hands



Avoid
Yuck
Touch
Wash
Clean
Safety
Pause
Short
Near
No
Slip
Dirty
Touch
Again

# 11. Conclude



Conclude

Discontinue

Ceasing, Ending, Closing

Cannot come back from this ending

Release

# 12. Time



A run that we lose no doubt
A fight that we lose when it's out

# 13. Failure



Failure
Disappointment
Losing, Stressing, Stumbling
Worked hard and did not meet the goal
Retry

# 14. Rules

Don't cut your hair
Don't ever swear
Don't gain more weight
Don't expect a mate

Don't talk to men
Don't ask me when
Don't speak your mind
Don't waste my time

Don't make me yell
Don't make me fight
Don't wear shorts
Don't watch sports

Don't disrespect me
Don't question me
Don't  degrade me
Don't embarrass me

Do what I say
Do it my way
Do know your place
Do follow rules

# 15. Okay



I am not okay
But I have to try
It is all smoke haze

On a Lost highway
A darkening sky
I am not okay

Stuck in a snow cave
As I just standby
I will be okay

Peace I will locate
Need I can't deny
I am not okay

My struggle showcase
Push myself to try
I will be okay

Forever, no way
Breath in, out a sigh
I am not okay
I will be okay

# 16. Push



Deepening sadness
And it will not go away
It has a tight grip
But I must push through the pain
There's light if i keep going

# 17. Heavy

I can feel it all and it's heavy to hold
Some days are grayer and it hurts me so deep
I'm met with a wall and around me is cold
Too many layers and the struggle is steep

One moment at a time is all I can take
Moving up I climb while I'm barely awake
Find the little joys that exist in each day
Ignoring all the noise I will find my way

# 18. Strong



I am strong
I am peace
I am love
I am smart

I am peace
I am brave
I am smart
I am bold

I am brave
I am fierce
I am bold
I am joy

I am fierce
I am smart
I am joy
I am strong

# 19. Beach



Breeze cool in my hair
Sun on my skin warm
Feet in the sand bare
Breeze cool in my hair
Peace like this so rare
Beach has me reborn
Sun on my skin warm

# 20. Reminders

Stand up tall with intent
Lower your shoulders down
Show you are confident
Head tall don't slip the crown
Keep your knees slightly bent
Steady walking around
Smile with good intent
Try to find common ground
Make the time here well spent

# 21. Life



Mindful
Youthful

Positive
Excitable
Assertive
Comical
Enthusiastic
Friendly
Unbothered
Loving

Lyrical
Imaginative
Faithful
Enchanting